D1236523

AS SLOW AS POSSIBLE

As Slow As Possible
Kit Fan

PUBLICATIONS
2018

Published by Arc Publications,
Nanholme Mill, Shaw Wood Road
Todmorden OL14 6DA, UK
www.arcpublications.co.uk

978 1911469 43 8 (pbk)
978 1911469 44 5 (hbk)
978 1911469 45 2 (ebk)

Design by Tony Ward
Printed in Great Britain by
TJ International, Padstow, Cornwall

Cover image:
Ffiona Lewis, *Golden Birch 2015*, Oil on Board, 116 x 151cm
© Ffiona Lewis

Editor for the UK & Ireland
John Wedgwood Clarke

for
Hugh Haughton

Forever is deciduous –
Except to those who die –

EMILY DICKINSON

You, her mother says watching her, are a migrant
of your own existence.

ALI SMITH

Time does not pass in the same way everywhere
in the world. In some places, it flows more quickly;
in others, more slowly.

CARLO ROVELLI

CONTENTS

Ɗ
GENESIS / 55

●
TWELVE MONTHS

○

TRANSMIGRATION

The day we saw a kingfisher on the Roman bridge of Salamanca
was the day we saw two otters on the bank of Rio Tormes in Salamanca

was also the day we saw the procession of Los Estudiantes in Salamanca
five days before Christ was supposed to have risen in Jerusalem

in the garden of Joseph of Arimathea where kingfishers and otters
were unlikely to have been seen. That sudden indigo is not to be mistaken

for cobalt, iceberg, peacock's crown or the poet's lapis lazuli.
Don't steal it, it says, *it is not for the human.* So bright it enters the mind

like greed, like a knife stabbing through once and quickly withdrawn
like a road accident happening at a distance you look at and drive

past. What does it mean, that living, spectral colour between blue
and violet, flying out of the arch, perching on the stone for three seconds

as the afternoon's running downstream? What would I barter for
this life? A man for a bird, or a stone for a pillow, except the thought

of you alive, or better still, *us* alive simultaneously, even once,
is enough. But just in case it's true, let's be the two otters.

ZURBARÁN'S WINDOW

I

There are midsummer days when the twenty-four
suns drink up all the wells in Fuente de Cantos.
Even the maps are eaten up by the shadows.

So, come along. Turn right, then left at the cul-de-sac
of a cobbled street. In the house of buttons, ribbons
and needles, the son of a haberdasher is drawing.

His hand says sky, and it turns charcoal blue.
His hand says clouds, and they turn charcoal rain.
His hand says mother, but she keeps sewing by the window.

II

Twenty-four years later, he looks into another window
where he puts a sewing basket by her ruby dress
and a single teardrop on her brooding face

as she sees her son braid a crown of thorns,
the matter-of-factness of his thumb teasing a thorn
out. A drop of blood on the index finger yet to be licked off

says God is in the detail. Slip in for a second.
Mind the salt glazed bowl by his bare feet. The window
in the house at Nazareth says it's raining in Fuente de Cantos.

THE NIGHT SWITCH

This is a sanctuary, you say, turning a page,
dotting the marginalia while my pixelated eyes
scan the news, weather, dust in Syria, soiling
the bed with white light pulsating through the night.
There's not enough darkness in the mind.
In the mind my mother's bleached, fluorescent hands
counting money, in the background the radio
humming the news, weather, Vietnamese refugees,
and me, lonely as a bird, swallowing the cry
of the jingling coins. She still does it every night,
counting, then, switching off the light in the corridor,
her silhouette glowing in the traffic as if on fire
and my mind hiding in the thicket of a burning tree.

SPILL

Man looking into the Earth
through the eye of satellite 'Terra' four days after the disaster mourning for
       the sea
wounded by a cloud of oil. No black tide from space but the waves
de-wrinkled by the stuff of life white as sperm. 'Oil smoothes the ocean,'
Michon Scott from NASA said, 'as a result, the oil slick is brighter
than the surrounding water.'
Pristine and effervescent, it wears the guise of
       holiness.
'Bright white ribbons', 'tendrils', 'the bird's-foot part of the delta',
Scott reports from Greenbelt, Maryland; his eyes glued to the flickering screen.
The metaphors we use to summon beauty to the place of terror,
say *Forgive them; for they know not what*
       they do.
Deepwater Horizon, like a colossal android from *Pacific Rim* reaching 30,000 feet
into the mantle,
       sank.
I do not know much about Hades but the suffering
we inflict on our own and other species is not unfamiliar to this blue
planet: pelicans drowned by the weight of their wings litter the coastline
with the bodies of ten thousand Icaruses, turtles smothered, bat-
       fish
wiped out, whale sharks blinded, dolphins hermit crabs sea grass
all glued to their charred unburned habitat like the souls in
       Phlegethon
swimming in a river of rust dark inflammable blood. It is human nature
to stand outside of a disaster
but you cannot stand outside of this. The microbes that eat the oil eat
oxygen eat fish eat animals eat roots eat the marshland.
There is no exit from
       COREXIT.

A species dies; a tree-branch shakes and snaps. There is nothing
to be forgiven or reconciled.
The photographs by Daniel Beltrá in *Spill* 'engender
a kind of "sublime melancholy", a reflection
of our current self-imposed alienation and careless neglect of our
         natural environment.'
A rush of rust red tracing the ridges of azure valleys like the shadow
of a shoal of anchovies swarming and dispersing in the silver lining
of a cloud or shimmering river-gods
punch-drunk at a new born estuary or Pollock's
         visceral constellations –
all the wrong words in the wrong places.

AMONG SCHOOL TEACHERS

The gate closed, bell unanswered, basketball court
stripped bare to lines and sparrows.
July is never the month for learning.

A school on Clear Water Bay Road, yet no water
bay, nor road. Through the Lotus-flowered Magnolias
a bridge I used to cross to the clamour of books.

A month of no children, but the translucent playground
after rain recalls the aftermath of hide-and-seek:
What's the time, Mr Wolf?

The tick-tocking knees,
the run for life. A boy under a tree
restless for the world to spin in ten seconds.

That summer day, among school teachers
we stood and sang.

Not of psalms and gospels but farewells and falling men:
How bodies became mountains.
How the wind knew of sadness, the soil
of love. The colour of blood was the colour of our flag.

In the assembly hall children who knew little of death
had seen images of guns and wounds, a speck
of a person stopping a column of tanks.

It was a clear day but we were all shut in.
The ground deserted to the democracy
of the sun.

The cicadas buzzing their way
to the dead of summer. The world waiting
under some tree.

A thousand souls still singing
in a dark assembly hall on Clear Water Bay Road.

ISCHIA

The day began in *La Mortella,* a garden named after the myrtle
for immortality but there was so much green life in it that death

was everywhere. The sky was a dead sea blue, the clouds a dead
silk white, and even the old Gingko adored by Goethe a dead

emerald green. What's in it for blue, white and green if death is not
in it? But it was the opposite that dazzled us. Now, tilt

your head a little, so that from this angle your face lights up like
the pearl lilies blazing in white flames against the pitch dark

blue shadows of protean ferns where giant green elephant ears
triumphantly rise. This is how I want to frame our time

on the island with you in it, among the blues, whites and greens:
if that day must come these colours will say *Don't be afraid.*

The dry day ended on rainless storm clouds as the dark
earth cowered under the white sparks, clean and quick

as dancing scythes. Heading for bed to read or make love
we were disrupted by the news from Ireland that the poet was dead.

All night the island rocked back and forth in its cradle like the final swing
of a coffin or the motion of a body travelling from one place

to another, with all the blues and whites and greens in your head
sleepwalking into a country where one thing ends and another begins.

MY MOTHER IN A VELÁZQUEZ

You were all blacks and shadows in the kitchen-darkness
where off-whites were still possible on some plates,

the brim of a mortar, a head of garlic sitting next to it
and a jug you seemed to have laid your full body weight on

so not to break it, as if breaking it here in this little town
called Emmaus would trigger something slightly unusual

like the breaking of bread which you might or might not have seen
in the background. You were smaller and larger than that,

being the one who had the chance to witness and hide away.
It was you, wasn't it? Though you were not that African,

that worrying look in the shadows of your brows
could only have been you, or at least how I or Velázquez

would have painted you, back in those days cleaning other peoples'
kitchens. I remember singing *Joyful, Joyful We Adore Thee* in Cantonese

I'd learned from a School Mass, when the houses were freed
of the hosts, when you turned the hoover to full blast.

My nose was caustic soda. I sang and sang and sang my heart
out. The house came clean. The air was deprived of dust.

MISTRAL

It comes at three and the Rhône runs
upstream. All the quay lamps disappear
by Pont du Trinquetaille at quarter past.

Those awake undream the long miles home
and those dreaming learn to walk again
as all glass turns back to breath and sand.

So much depends upon the undoing
that the five loaves and two fishes
are left untouched, undivided.

So much depends upon the light of Arles
that the sun and sea are reborn
as new planets of yellow and blue.

But what's done is undone:
the Rhône downstream, lamps ablaze.
The ominous is nothing but a backward miracle.

Twelve baskets of leftovers.
A bandaged ear, and what seems to be Mount Fuji.
When it goes, there is a great calm.

LES ALYSCAMPS

The mistral drops
    and what returns to the ground returns
    to dust. The poplars rise among the pines and yews
    to a green September vista. Trees
    that come from shadows turn to shadows.
I retrace
    your footsteps forty-six years ago with salt
    of the Camargue coating your skin. You saw a boy
    rolling a hoop along a disused railway line. You
    were eighteen and I had no age.
We saunter
    through the road of open tombs, unnamed
    by their weathered stones. Here a trace of Adam hiding
    in the leaves and there a firstborn dangling
    from a sword. Christ was here once, attending a funeral.
We descend
    to an empty nave tongue-tied by the coo coo
    of pigeons and the eek of bats. Not a single soul
    in sight, yet there seems to be another among us
    teetering in the dark at that thin border.
The bats shave
    past our spines, homing in the open air
    as the road winds itself into dusk. We pick ourselves up
    from the ground, heading on to the other end
    for it is toward evening, and the day is far spent.

TREES AFTERWARDS

After the unlayering of clothes, entwining of arms, tiptoeing
about on fingertips, there comes a kind of sound
sleep stolen from lovemaking

in which you alone were found
under the bracken shades by the River Shournagh
in your throne improvising a universe with twigs and branches

known to the local pike, minnows, mosquitos and Buddleia
while I was found alone in a different tranche
of time with my head stuck

in a tree hole, bee in my ear
puzzled by the city's green life in Victoria Park.
We wake to find the park concreted over, the majestic beeches at the rear

of your parents' house gone like them. But the two trees hold.
As the bark grew, their lips were sealed.

TO THE SHADOW-MILLIONS

In response to the People's Republic of China State Council's White
Paper, *"The Practice of the 'One Country, Two Systems' Policy in the Hong
Kong Special Administrative Region"* (June 2014)

This is what happens.
On a wind-changing, moonless night the plugs
are pulled and the Earth-proud skyline
drops.

In pitch-dark occupancy
the shadow-millions hum
in black unison, black as hair as
pupils as everything else in the dark with no eyes.

What do the shadows remember?
Not the fireworks.
Not the laser beams.
Not the moth in fire chasing its own shadow.

The candles, the candles, they say,
thousands of them, lit this one June day.
But of course no questions asked.
And no eyes answering.

AS SLOW AS POSSIBLE

Having breathed six hundred and thirty-nine years,
what remains of us will return to St. Burchardi
in Halberstadt, the hometown of the first permanent
pipe organ, in the six hundred and fortieth year
of the third millennium, whether or not Earth
has been forsaken. The exact month, date and time
are yet to be confirmed, but we, stranger still,
will gather in the right transept, first to listen
to that last note sustained by sandbags on pedals,
its ghostly, peculiar ring in the ear reminding us
of ourselves; then, if breath can still be held,
to witness the sandbags being gently removed
all at once, so that this time, we can hear the finished
sound, the tinnitus recalling absence.

RESISTANCE

There comes a time a leaf will furl back to its vein
with generations of green mouths unbudding
as a form of protest, a way of branching in.

And there will be no rustling where the wind has been
and many a limb in the fall will not have gone missing.
There comes a time a leaf will furl back to its vein

and twigs and branches will unfork and loosen
their ties. No more dappled streets, no healing
of the nations, as the crowns are branching in.

Each bark-year withdraws and each ring loses its kin.
Each strand of root retraces its course into nothing.
There comes a time a leaf will furl back to its vein.

It will return to the first acorn within
a family of seeds, leaving no trace of its undoing,
a quiet protest, a way of branching in.

It will return to where it once survived and begin
again in the valley of its unmaking.
There comes a time a leaf will furl back to its vein
as a form of protest, a way of branching in.

TEN HAIKUS BY FAN KUAN

for Adam Phillips and Judith Clark

Dusk –
at the spine of a cliff some warblers singing –
Oh it's dawn.

Mountains
of good ink
seen through tracing paper.

Treetops dampen
cloudily
like pubic hair.

Pine needles
whistle
at clouds end.

A fingernail of waterfall:
the first lightning
this early spring.

Mists arguing
with drizzles deciding
which is which.

Wood smoke,
a hilltop monastery,
    a thin rice broth!

        Midnight –
    even the spring crickets
        are making love.

    Fishes flick up
in the drizzle;
    I pee discreetly.

        Why sleep
    when the new moon is blinking
        elsewhere?

THE RIVER VIENNE

for Hélène Lecossois and Lionel Pilkington

Like a boy-arrow homing to a hidden place
you and your mandarin orange shirt plunge
into the green-yellowing edge of summer
holidays where a mud path disappears
into the noughts and crosses of beech-roots
on the secret meandering tongue of *La Vienne.*

No one speaks. Not even the river-god busily
being a river and a god. A tree lets the wind
steal a branch or the branch finds a way to leave
the tree for a life of shimmer. A stone is turned
or imagined turning, like the unheard *'or'* sound
of wise ghost-fishes who delight in water.

When you're found in plain sight under the crescent
of a commuter-railway bridge, you're far from lost.
The air is a handful of *trompettes de la mort,*
the musky rundown rooms of an inherited
château, turned dormitory. The visitors are long
gone but their greyish absence smells like a river.

The trick is not in the beginning or the end, the tip of the tongue or the mouth of
      the anus,
but the muddle in-between called 'life'. Life in a *homo signorum*
on a folded vellum almanac showing the body-zodiac: Scorpion on his heart,
his feet surfing on Pisces. Life in the wound-man from an *Apocalypse*:
a spear through the skull, an arrow in the groin, a knife-opened
      arm
and the legend in German reading, 'Ich bin das Alpha und das Omega,
der Erste und der Letzte.' Life in the vein of Galen
in the eyes of an English wound-man staring out like a Barbary macaque
mourning for the forest. Life in an ivory model of a pregnant woman
whose removable body parts reveal a miniature
      foetus
used by midwives to offer reassurance. Life in an unlikely fugitive sheet
showing Eve's parted legs, with flaps raised to show her labelled vagina.
Life in another fugitive engraving of 1566 imagining
partium corporis humani, all internal organs piled up like a black forest
gâteau. Life as a house in *The Work of Tobias* where
      the eyes
are windows, the mouth is a door and the brain has numerous
attic rooms. Life in the eyes of Paolo Mascagni in forty-four hand-
coloured plates where the heart sees its first
      epicardium
removed to disclose its muscular engine. Life in *Gray's Anatomy* beginning
with a dedication to Benjamin Brodie 'in admiration of his great talents,
and in remembrance of many acts of kindness
shown to the author.' Life in my early memory of a Brödel illustration
of a circumcised penis on the wall as I opened my
      mouth
and said 'ARRRRRGH' while the family doctor pressed my tongue
with an ice lolly stick bone-dry as the Sahara desert.
      Life
in the eleventh hour still lingering in Arezzo where the fading Adam
is seated naked by a rock among his offspring and Eve with her sagging

breasts smoothes the back of his head as the story is told
over and over again: from the seed of the first apple springs
        the tree
of the cross rustling in the wind where a generation of green mouths
passes secret messages to one another
like Chinese whispers.

THE BURNING OF BOOKS

'Anyone under the Skies who has copies of the Classic of Poetry, the Classic of History, or the writing of the Hundred Schools of Thought shall hand them out for burning. Anyone who has failed to burn the books thirty days after this announcement shall be sent to build The Great Wall.'

'The Basic Annals of the First Emperor of Qin' (213 BC),
Records of the Grand Historians

Some said the sky had fallen, the sun
didn't rise, some said lightning followed
thunder, walls were built without roofs,
and some said nothing at all and nothing
mattered for someone deaf as an adder.

Each day I put the horse before the cart,
walked door to door along the Wei river
where a mile of dust brought a ton of books.

At midday I sat by the banks, had lunch
while the horses munched away in the grass.

I walked and walked till the mud track
deepened ten inches under the wheels.

Then I stopped and piled them up as instructed
into loose towers, letting them breathe
in air, since bamboo burns hot but not for long.

I watched the newly-written more fibrous
ones giggle and pop like fireworks
and the old ones dither into the night

while ember-tinted thoughts whispered
to each other like orphans behind closed doors.

I found my hands fishing in the lukewarm
ashes for odd pieces of charred words,
each staring black like a horse's eye
till I dropped them into an empty well.

Then I saw heaps of smudged, wounded faces
tongue-tied in that half-lit mouth.

I let them be, sealed the lid, put the cart
before the horse, and walked the mile home.

DON KOWLOON

If *hunger is the best sauce*
           in the world, pour it over
me, fill this gulf (that they call

harbour) dividing them and
           us, free this island from mi-
rage and make it poor again.

A single tread of my arm-
           oured foot could drown this giant sea
turtle exhibition of

shared capital on a piece
           of land borrowed from a
granite hill rising from the

sea, changing from hand to hand
           between those with tattoos and
those with cufflinks underneath

a tailored suit. I shall rise
           against the neon canons,
toughened glass mills, serial dis-

appearances like the man
           in yesterday's paper and
gas-tears dripping off the brims

of the yellow umbrellas.
           This peninsula named
after the nine dragons I

struck down has long been part of
        the Pearl Delta but dragons
like faxes are long gone and

fireworks are no substitute.
        Life here is transitory
though I find society

in the trees of Lion Rock,
        the birds of Tolo Harbour
and a day will come when I

find a stone with my name on
        it. Until then it is what
it is. No Rocinante

now. I lost him to Happy
        Valley, and Sancho, my old
companion, where are you?

EUROPA

It seems an abstract pattern
            like Ptolemy's early borders,
            a historical conundrum,
a white bull horn and resolute
            will to power in the name of

stability and union.
            In the shallow waves of Tyre
            the boisterous hooves wait, drawing
in the shallow waves. Desperate
            times call for desperate measures, says

Hippocrates, but time is kill
            or cure, a technocratic
            conjurer with a homemade scythe
who runs around the city clocks
            reaping the whirlwind for the stock.

The great god, now compromised,
            requires a change of heart, frantic
            understanding from his broken
counterpart. The scene's not the one
            with Rubens' flying cherubim

but Rembrandt's sunlit encounter
            where the knots of apparitions
            are tied to those who're left behind.
The trophy carried on the back
            of the bull is the face of fright

and submission. The goddess will
            survive as long as the idea
            of it survives, in the midnight
oil, in the hearts of its people,
            in books, statues, and museums.

A TREE ORDAINED

'A tree's grown inwards / from my temples.'
OCTAVIO PAZ, 'A Tree Within'

Smoked herring-leaves hanging
on fallen branches on maggot-white
ember-soil. Five barefoot monks
walking on wood-corpses. Ash-snow
falling in Cardamom Forest and there is
nothing inward about devastation.

In Areng valley wild grasses half as tall
as elephants glistened like emeralds
after downpours and down the steep
elephant corridor Siamese crocodiles
bathed in grassy rivers where the scales
of wild fish shimmered in the eddies.

Saffron-robed, the last unfellable one
stands ordained like a cenotaph
for the aurochs, quagga, dodo.
Wind-voices from the burnt, about-to-be-
submerged villages saying *let's
leave our tree and sell our buffalo.*

IN CRETE

Four thin monkeys, well-trained saffron-gatherers
half-faded on the fresco are still picking the sunbeams

from the crocuses in the field. A mother of pearl necklace
Sossina once owned is buried with her stillborn child.

The first true glass from the northern coast of Syria
arrived in a small village and here it stands

a greenish vase; though its mouth is chipped, its body
is clear as water. I come here for a modest procession:

a stone frame drum, a couple of fipple flutes
and a reed dulcian, an ancestor of the bassoon,

people sobbing and murmuring, sounds
of human grief. That silent pause when the body

is carried to the opened ground, whispers
of shovelled earth, the odd birdcall, the humming

of a well. Since death is local and ceremonial,
music, food and wine have lasted into the dead

of night when the Great Dipper quenches its thirst
in the well. The cicadas are gone, branches barely stirred.

Persephone is packing up for the coming months.
Nobody notices the beginning of autumn.

A CHAIR FROM BUDDHA MOUNTAIN

for Kabbie Ngo

I was born in the seventh year of the second millennium
up the Pearl River Delta in the city of Foshan – Buddha

Mountain – where two-third of the world's chairs are born
every year in my hometown. I belong to the family of patio

chairs, a tough, durable breed made to withstand the Cretan
sun and Aberdeenshire gales. Wicked things were said about

me before I arrived. With plastic skin and a steel heart, I imitate
cane, reed or bamboo, an improved descendant of wicker.

I had a difficult birth in the coldest winter in recent history
when one of my thousand mothers worked sixteen hours a day

through Christmas, their hands half-frozen, purple with bruises
and green with cuts, weaving me into shape. I have a heart

of steel, remember? I heard them cursing my longevity,
my skin harder than my younger brothers' a year ago.

They sobbed too among themselves, the little they earned
for my living. It was a bad winter; the temperature dropped

below zero. Frostbitten hands finally went on strike. Someone
rang someone in Hong Kong who rang someone in Britain.

Then photographs were taken of those hands and someone
told someone in Britain that my birth had to be delayed.

Here I am, in an alleyway off Bird Street near Selfridges
battered like the hands of my mothers, having only spent

two years in this corner kingdom. If you ask me where I
come from, I could tell you stories about my kind, about antiquity

and simplicity: the Pharaohs, the Tang, how the privilege
of sitting became an ordinary thing, and how Vincent

van Gogh remembered us. If you had time, I would tell
you about the beautiful mountains of Foshan where a Tripitaka

Master from Kashmir brought two bronze Buddhas
to my hometown and placed them on the highest cliff

for the locals' first temple. That was three hundred
and ninety-eight years into the first millennium. Religion

was still young. I was there too, in an earlier form.
There weren't many of us in those days and I was stone.

FILIAL PIETY

The tree wants to be still.

The wind doesn't.

THE OTHER HALF

for Polly Yuen and Trevor Throntveit

It's hard to imagine it the other way round:
    two faces on opposite sides of the same head
cartwheeling down the first hill with eight
    limbs living in one being as a simple sphere
to share the same lungs and stomach
    to have the penis and vagina so conveniently
close to each other to worship flux all the time
    to be the moon and share the same anus.

Then it starts again with the yearning for the cut
    like a single cell in pitch dark waiting to split.
The breaks, the rows, the ambiguities the he-
    art clarified to make things glow. And to
this day, sliced like a flatfish, two out of
    one, each learns to perfect the embrace, hold-
ing hands, finishing each other's sentences

43

LAW OF DESIRE

for Agnes Lam

After hours on the economies of scale and random
variables, you arrived and summoned Proteus
as the verb *to be*: noting how among the seals Menelaus
caught the lion, serpent, leopard or water,
or how it changes its form in different tenses
and the way English grammar is brick and mortar
for clear articulation of thought, even about boredom.

To thirty-three slumberous dreamers, the answer
was recess. But there was a black sheep susceptible
to the instability of things who found the god adorable
in a library corner, pondering on the muscles.
You were amazed at that raw curiosity comparable
to a hunger unlikely in the hustle and bustle
of this disowned city on the cusp of the Handover.

So against the curriculum you fed him poems. Between lessons
you left the daffodils and clouds, and frost at midnight
deep in his desk drawer out of sight.
Books that moved you blossomed again in the hands
of a secret sharer who in time learned to recite
the odd line, toying with such puzzles in his mind
as a burning tiger that has no rhyme or reason.

One day during recess you gave him a parcel
and whispered, 'watch it when your parents are asleep.'
He went on to burn the midnight oil until they were deep
in the land of Nod. His first Almodóvar,
a name he couldn't pronounce, made his heart leap
forward across the embarrassing teenage years, over
to the other shore. Like Jacob, he learned to wrestle.

BRUEGHEL'S TREES

There was a time when we were not here.
Not stirring the primal scene, not stealing the thunder
from some god. Time when time passed
more slowly for birds.

A web of super-surveillance where the trees
had ears and fields had eyes. The glint
in an owl's eyes flashing on the bark-stigmata
waiting for a Thomas to testify.

And winter sharp as a knife-edge came
cutting throats. No more children, horses, mothers'
praying hands. Just a pool of dead water,
a frozen branch fallen, as if we weren't here.

Same pack of dogs returned from the hunt;
same fox and pig eaten. The landscape standing
white; the empty crowns frigid. Hail to the magpie
who could see no ski and cart, no ball games.

So much pageantry to undo – the plough,
wings, splash – that even the spring leaves
turned a blind eye to worms and the sun,
to whatever information came closest to the truth.

BANKSY IN GAZA

Has art a place in this ruined corner of Beit Lahiya
where children in oversized shoes bring water home

in plastic bottles, running as if chased by shadows
along the grey concrete wall greened by tough weeds

on bone-dry sand, the traffic of their footprints
written and overwritten all day like a game

except there is no fun in playing thirsty or filthy
this February, or any month for that matter

while as they run their shadows run on the wall
among the six painted children flying sky high

on a watch-tower turned carnival-swing, feet dancing
in the open air like the blue, cursive Arabic letters

lapping on a forbidden shore, what is imaginary,
the black paint like the flammable tar that coloured the tower,

the swing, the flying children fading in the heat of the sun,
or the small shadows running back and forth for water,

or the long wall of teeth and eyes and ears –
how should we unimagine a thing once it's been imagined?

DUODENUM

For over a decade, my father came home a failed man.
A shadow of himself, he would take off his tired shoes,
crack open a false smile and collapse in bed like a half-
crushed worm. He would curl up and hug his wife's
pillow close to his chest. On the worst days, he shut the door
to keep the trouble of the twelve finger-breadths to himself.

That was how I learned to cook: rinsing grains of tear-like
rice over a cold tap till my hand went numb, slicing
a tenderloin of pork, heading and tailing a red mullet.
I was ten, at most. In the end, he would emerge
from his cocoon, turn on the gas, throw in what seemed
a life sizzling in a wok. And I would stand and keep watch.

THE PAINTED GARDEN IN THE VILLA OF LIVIA

for Louise Ho

A perpetual spring where Persephone has not left
        but you've left. Earth is young and spirits

numerous: a half-eaten pomegranate will not
        rot, an oriole on encountering the red underworld-

fruit will still its beak in yellow puzzlement,
        like its neighbour-swallow, tilting above

some golden quinces, still undecided whether to land
        or not to land, or this blackbird caught black-handed

alighting from the cloud-edge of a holm-oak leaf.
        It must be difficult to imagine a flightless existence

when everything flowers and fruits at the same
        time. Come closer, Livia. These blue-white traces,

like you, aren't phosphorescence. Why look
        at the walls when the world is far and wide? *The heat*

you said, *the scorching heat that burns the seas,*
        pointing at the only caged bird perching on the garden

wall, a shadow of a bird, species-less, like our time.
        You ask me to take a piece of the white-blue sky

from this flightless thing and *walk away with it.*
        So I've taken it and I'm walking away with it.

TWO MINDS

First it was the waiting, then the walking.
Summer, under the white-mulberry tree, white
sarcophagi and half-crushed worms, some green
figments like Adam's leaf. Two boys
waiting for each other secretly, walking
home together. Just walking as in silk-making,
so much growing happening all at once.
The smell of sea salts from new underarm hair.

Those were the hours you emerged from your shy
cocoon, building future-variations not unlike
Lego-blocks: a love-foundation, the career-ladder,
a sky-light roof where Orion rises while you
and the ideal anonymous female are embracing,
kissing. Unkissed like so many, we spoke of
different kinds of kissing, the river-tongue.
You wanted two children, boy and girl,
rhyming with man and wife. A rounded
prospect, a circle where every point contributed
to the matter of life with little deviation:
minimal damage, faint imperfections.

So many structures to listen to I became
Chaos, unmaker of shapes like the green wind
flowing through the summer leaves, not bothered
if it was indeed the wind itself or water or an absent-
minded contentment which had nothing to do with
anything. Not knowing became a form of feeling
but I did know and not know your half-buttoned shirt,
the gentle valley of your chest, the way you parted your hair
and the wind unparted it, the salt running down
to the ridge of your lips unreachable by any tongue,
the growing chasm, a landscape where your mountains
and my rivers would be continents apart.

TEN YEARS

Timing is the working in perfect unison of arms
when a hug intimates sleep, is every Sunday
afternoon rewinding a grandfather clock that's lost its chime,
is the tongue starting and stopping
an argument, is lovemaking, is the wren singing

when we lie casually awake at four in the morning
listening to one lucky heart eavesdropping
on another as in early days. Our timing was a double mime,
a dissolving marriage, and the way
you tilted that hat, walking in with your tentative charm.

MIGRANT

for Ziad Elmarsafy

Months have passed and we have seen enough of death
this winter that even though seeing these chlorophyll

green leaves suckle on the sun again and tower over Russell Square
broadcasting *C'est la vie* on this one June day aren't enough

for the sea-deaths, land-deaths and air-deaths un-extinguishing
somewhere else, not yet out-of-sight, out-of-mind. Not yet *here* too,

this corner kingdom we've elected to live within still seemingly
prospers like the summer holm-oak by the Hotel Russell

you'll come to frequent in your new life in the capital.
People lazing about in the sun as in *La Grande Jatte*, children shrieking

in the fountain, a father carrying his bum-bare boy on his shoulders,
an old couple walking past, catching our eye, still walking

past. *So many of us, I want to know every single life, what
brought them here today, who they are, and how long they will live.*

We all have it, living it, re-living it, shaping this one-off malleable
thing over and over that even though all winter we've seen

what could happen to it, we still sit on the bench among the perishable
green, chattering about it as if it won't leave us just like that.

51

GENESIS

CHAPTER 1

In the beginning there was nothing.

2 And the sky and the land were muddled like an unhatched egg.

盤古 3 And Pangu lived in the egg.

4 And in darkness he lived, for eighteen thousand years.

5 And slowly the sky and the land divided.

6 And the place that was clouded became the sky.

7 And the place that was cloudless became the land.

8 And Pangu lived between the clouded and the cloudless.

9 And each day came nine metamorphoses.

10 And each day the sky grew by one foot.

11 And each day the land grew by one foot.

12 And each day Pangu grew by one foot.

13 And another eighteen thousand years passed.

14 And the sky was higher, the land deeper, and Pangu taller.

15 And there were nine thousand miles between the sky and the land,

三皇
五帝 long before the arrival of the Three Sovereigns and Five Emperors.

16 And Pangu grew old and died.

17 And from his breath the wind blew, from his voice thunder muttered, from his left eye the sun shone, and from his right eye the moon waxed.

18 And his body sketched the contours of all terrains. And from his blood the rivers flowed, from his nerves the fault-lines met, and from his muscles the soil formed.

19 And from his hair the constellations ran, from his skin the woods whistled, from his teeth the precious metals formed, from his spine the pearls were pried open, and from his sweat the rain poured.

20 And the insects learned the lessons of the wind and their labours enriched the first soil.

CHAPTER 2

Thus the sky and the land flourished, and all the host of them.

2 And there was no trace of human beings.

3 And the goddess Nüwa appeared 女媧 with Fu Xi, her brother and husband. 伏羲

4 And they had the face of humans, but the body of serpents.

5 And Nüwa wandered the lonesome sky and the lonesome land, and pitied their lonesomeness.

6 And she learned the lessons of the wind, planted her hands in the yellow river, held the earth, and said, Let us make humans in our image, after our likeness.

7 So she created humans in her image, moulded the earth into shapes, without detail or features.

8 And her pace was slow, and so many died before they lived.

9 So Nüwa fed a reed into the wet earth, flicked it high with her arm, and turned the earth into the living.

10 Although her pace was quicker, the human beings that she made were without detail or features.

風 11 So Nüwa employed the *wind* which divided men and women, drew their faces, and gave them limbs.

12 And with the help of the wind, lo the reed flew sky-high and Nüwa's labours multiplied seventyfold.

13 And Nüwa saw the living she had made, and beheld that it was good.

14 But human beings too were lonesome creatures. Without language, men and women did not know how to love and care for each other.

15 And Nüwa borrowed the language of the wind, plucked reeds, bound them into vertical pipes, and created an instrument.

笙 She called it *sheng*, the living.

16 And she taught men and women to borrow the language of the wind which was the language of music which was the language of love.

17 And men and women used the fifty chords of *sheng* for their emotions.

18 And where there was music, there was harmony among the living.

19 And Nüwa saw the men and women who spoke in harmony with the wind, and she granted them a new way of living, a union of two called wedlock.

20 And Nüwa learned the lessons of the wind, and heard the happy and sad music of men and women who were once a grain of earth on a hollow reed.

CHAPTER 3

Now as men and women fell in love in the songs of *sheng*, Fu Xi noticed that the instrument itself was alone.

2 So Fu Xi borrowed the language of the air which was the language of the wind. He found a hollow tree, picked five strands of his long hair, and fed them through the wood as strings.

3 And harmony was found in the lightest of touches. And he called it *qin*, a companion of *sheng*. 琴

4 And Fu Xi taught men and women to borrow the language of the air which was the language of touch which was the language of love.

5 And men and women spoke the language of love when they could, through the conversations of *sheng* and *qin*.

6 And one day Fu Xi traced the scales on the fish to sew a net, and cast it upon the seas and rivers, and

lo fish were caught in abundance.

7 And he taught the living the habit of the net, and the rule of modesty.

8 And one day Fu Xi sat on the highest mountain, far from the noises of the living.

9 And he gazed at the mutability of the sky and wrestled with the fixity of the land.

10 And like a stranger, he pondered the variety of birds and animals, how they communed with the sky and the land that they were part of.

11 And Fu Xi listened to the lessons of the wind which were the lessons 水 of the *waters*.

12 And where there was nearness to his own being, there was distance from what he beheld and owned.

13 And after many days and many nights on the highest mountain, listening to the lessons of the wind and water, he saw a pattern in his mind's eye, an octagon which encompassed the mutability and fixity of all things.

14 And it was all before the beginning of ideas and thoughts, and before the beginning of the mind and its objects.

15 And he drew down what he thought he saw in his mind and made it into a real object, and his 八卦 descendants called it *bagua*, an instrument of thoughtfulness and thoughtlessness which read the brokenness and unbrokenness

of all things, and which was the beginning of *yin* and *yang*.　陰陽

16 And with *bagua* Fu Xi observed the seasons and constellations.

17 And with *bagua* Fu Xi predicted the feet of the rain, the shadows of the storm, the labours of the sun, and the phases of the moon.

18 And with *bagua* Fu Xi recorded the first spring when the insects awakened, the first summer when the cicadas sang and fell, the first autumn when the dews were white, and the first winter when frost descended upon the earth.

19 And Fu Xi kept all the records in order, from the first to the last, which was the first calendar and the beginning of time.

20 And henceforth the living lived and died, in the beginning of time and in the end of time.

CHAPTER 4

This is the book of the generations of men and women, when the living multiplied under the face of the sky and on the face of the land, and when sons and daughters were born unto good and bad husbands and wives.

2 And the good men and women lived and died, and the bad men and women lived and died, and there was the same destination for the good and the bad.

3 And for years the living respected

the waters out of fear and the fire out of affection.

共工
祝融
4 And so Gong Gong, the god of water, was jealous of Zhu Rong, the god of fire.

5 And Gong Gong gathered all the waters from the Five Lakes and Four Seas to flood Kunlun Mountains, the

崑崙山
sacred home of Zhu Rong.

6 And without fire, darkness descended on the face of land, and the living died in plague and fear.

7 And Zhu Rong, fired with anger, rode on flames and fought with Gong Gong on Kunlan Mountains.

8 But it was the nature of water to flow downhill, and in burning flames, Gong Gong lost the battle and retreated in shame.

9 And Gong Gong in his anger smashed his head against Buzhou

不周山
Mountain, a pillar holding up the sky.

10 And the pillar fell, the sky broke and tilted towards the northwest, the land faulted and shifted to the southeast, the water prevailed, and the mountains were covered.

11 And Nüwa saw that all in whose nostrils was the breath of life died, and every living substance was destroyed which was under the face of the sky and on the face of the land, and every creeping thing disappeared.

12 And so Nüwa wandered the Five Lakes and Four Seas, and every

corner of the land, and found the last surviving mountain above water, carried on the back of the turtle Ao.

鰲

13 And Nüwa borrowed the fire from the sun and it took her nine days and nights to refine the rocks of the last mountain into thirty-six thousand five hundred and one stones, and each stone had five different colours.

14 And for nine days and nights Nüwa used thirty-six thousand and five hundred stones to repair the broken sky.

女媧補天

15 And one stone was left on the top of the last surviving mountain.

16 But the seamless sky without its pillars was falling down, and so Nüwa broke the feet of the turtle Ao, and used them as pillars to hold the falling sky.

17 And to save the last mountain from sinking, Nüwa carried it to a place in the East Sea, which descendants called the City of the Sun.

18 And behold the sky and the land were now repaired and balanced, the rain from the sky was restrained, and the waters were abated from the land.

19 And the tops of mountains were seen from afar, and every beast, and every creeping thing, and every fowl returned.

20 And the generations of men and

women returned under the face of the sky, on the face of the land, and there were untold generations to come.

CHAPTER 5

For the mouths of the living multiplied, the fowls of the sky dwindled, the animals of the land declined, and the variety of plants diminished.

神農 2 And Shennong, the Divine Farmer and the God of Medicine, wandered through the depleted land and saw the suffering of the creatures.

3 And Shennong had an ox head, sharp horns, bronze forehead, iron skull, four human limbs, and a transparent body which showed his heart, lungs, stomach, liver, and guts.

4 And Shennong wandered to the nearest and furthest forests on the face of the land, tasted all plants and 嘗百草 herbs, and recorded their good and ill natures.

5 And when the plants and herbs were of good nature, they glowed in his transparent body like a rainbow; and when the plants and herbs were of ill nature, they darkened in his transparent body like a storm.

6 And from the weather of his body Shennong deciphered and recorded the tempers of all plants and herbs.

7 And Shennong taught men and women to borrow the language of plants and herbs which was the language of attention which was the language of cure.

8 But the men and women who fell ill and recovered still suffered, for there was not enough food for the mouths of the living.

9 And Shennong retreated to the forest, and listened to the lessons of the wind in the breath of *sheng* and the lessons of the air in the touch of *qin*.

10 And he dug his hands in the soil, and learned the lessons of growth which were the lessons of furrows made by the labours of worms and insects.

11 And Shennong borrowed the confidence of the tree, and bowed a branch into the shape of the waves which was the shape of the moon.

12 And lo the soil responded to the waves and the moon, and in the first furrow came the first of seed.

13 And Shennong stood in the furrowed land, beheld that it was good, and he named the hoe. 耒耜

14 And Shennong taught men and women to borrow the language of furrows which was the language of the hoe which was the language of growth.

15 And from the nobility of fingers came the rake, and from the 鏟 determination of arms came the spade. 耙

16 And from the simplicity of the

鎌
犁 hoe came the plough, and from the
efforts of sweat came the sickle.

17 And the generations of men and
women learned the lessons of the
land, and taught their sons and
daughters the lessons of growth
which were the lessons of humility
which were the lessons of the hoe.

18 And the first seeds germinated
under the face of the sky and on the
天地 face of land.

19 And the first seeds flowered
in the labours of sun and rain,
pollinated in the labours of the wind
and bees, fertilised in the labours
of chance, fruited in the labours
of time, seeded in the labours of
continuity, and preserved in the
labours of the hand.

20 And the living learned the seven
ages of the seed which were the
seven ages of men and women, in
the beginning of time and in the end
of time.

TWELVE MONTHS

of the front door yet to be repainted
probably this spring in Hague blue; of
the porch door newly painted in a draft-
washed white; of the kitchen door ajar
smell of a pork shoulder roasting in garlic
and fennel seeds; of the cat flap reserved
for the sleek, handsome Pantalaimon
and regally neurotic Aphrodite; of
concrete and abstract things like change
passages
        transitions
                like climbing up
the stairs to discover the things within
human control like frame within frame
the variations of blue and sea that make
the beak of a hummingbird fit for a curlew
and the things beyond like an unexpected
phone call on a Sunday morning, disrupted
lovemaking, the loss and tears that follow,
thoughts of exit and entrance clouding over
the mind on a cold sunny day where everything has a shadow to make meaning of.

The Irish Times Family Notices, 23rd January, Haughton (Carrigrohane)

B. Alan (former Chairman and CEO of Haughtons Ltd, and member of the Irish Davis Cup team). Dearly loved husband of the late Betty and dear father of Jane, Peter, Hugh, David and Richard, remembered with love and admiration by his children, grandchildren, great-grandchildren, daughters-in-law, son-in-law, sister-in-law Jean Witherington, brother-in-law Hugh Knox, as well as nieces, nephews and friends of all ages. Funeral Service in The Society of Friends Meeting House, Summerhill South, Cork on Saturday January 29, at 11 o'clock Family flowers only. Donations to Amnesty International or Cork Penny Dinners. c/o Patricia Bogan. O'Connor Bros, North Gate Bridge. Cork.

TWO DREAMS

Two dreams like two trees entwined
on an uneven bed: one Kafkasque,
a courthouse full of eyes, the charge
unknown, sentence unannounced;
the other Borgesian, upstairs, three cats,
one with red stripes, downstairs, things
tilting nautically, windows opening
to waves.
        Of course, it can't just be
about theories and repetitions.
The soul must also learn to sing like
this pendulum rumbling through
the night while the gilded clock
face keeps its lips sealed.
           It wants to say
everything that has been said before
but it goes without saying that the night
is still young, the leaves are unfurling,
you and I, ass to ass, humming our own
hymn to hide-and-seek, into the woods,
behind the trees, among the undergrowth.

Model Specification: Mahogany Norfolk Clock, dial signed A Merga, Nantwich,
two train, 8-day movement with anchor escapement rack striking on a saucer bell.

STRIPPING IVY

Late March, the sky the underside
of a Dover sole. An allusion to rain
lingering in the soil.
                        The mind
keeps pottering at unfinished
work while the hands are purposeful
when they come to potting –
thyme, sage, rosemary, accompanied
by a winter-burnt bay: a kitchen
larder new to the plain old yard.
North-facing in semi-shade,
which parts will get the sun
are yet to be learned. But life
has to start somewhere and *Tess*
of the D'Urbervilles, A Shropshire Lad –
roses named after great books –
will they thrive?
                        The deep-rooted
climber, home to blue finches,
robins, earthworms and woodlice,
has been plotting in the dark,
and may not think so.

Characteristics according to David Austin: Tess of the D'Urbervilles. Climbing, English Old Hybrid, Crimson, Strong Fragrance, Repeat Flowering, 10ft, 1998, Appellation AUSMOVE; A Shropshire Lad. Climbing, English Leander Hybrid, Peachy Pink, Strong Fragrance, Repeat Flowering, 10ft, 1996, Appellation AUSLED.

DOUBLESPEAK

for Anna Armstrong

Early April, some greening syllables
are jostling their way through
the drizzly soil.
                    The convivial
whisperings of those little mouths
are sustained at their own pace
without repetition, hesitation
or deviation,
                    until, in just a minute
the sun comes out of the blue and says
nothing, leaving the conversation
with a shade of slight equivocation.

Ian Cassan Messiter (2 April 1920 – 22 November 1999). THE GUARDIAN OBITUARIES: 'At Sherborne school he was once caught day-dreaming during a lesson on Henry VIII and his wives. The master, who was fond of using the cane, slammed it on a desk beside Messiter's ear and demanded that he talk for two minutes on what he had just been talking about or face the cane. He once said that his preferred epitaph would be simply that he helped to broaden people's minds.'

SHELVING AND HAILING

for Geoffrey Weaver

Whether the weather will settle
does not matter to a self-shelved
mind, nor to the precarious level
where the spirit lies.
                    Like a snail
carrying its library in the aisles
of Babel, poetry too reluctantly
depends on the space it occupies
and the objects it possesses.
The song of a Black & Decker
however crude has its twists
and turns. Has it gone in?
Is it flush? Questions that beg
answers when the unevenness
of joinery on the whole tells
of a lifetime's achievement –
spine after spine of books
of long and short poems
in their boxes, half a million
pages untouched, unturned
for months, impatient.
Outside, the clouds thick
with hailstones are equally
impatient.
              The sash window
on the other hand leisurely
frames a young blackbird
sitting among the camp pink
cherry branches, discreetly
calling, 'May', 'May', 'May'.

Measurement: 247H x 235W, to fit Bishop's *Collected Prose* with a fingerbreadth
spare, to just fit *Early Auden* and Zukofsky's *Catullus*, and to fit Niedecker's *Collected
Poems 1968* with a light squeeze.

ELDER

for Mimi Ching

In the mind of clouds, the intimate
difference in age is to a large extent
a shady business.
                    Each minute
it lectures publicly on the sixty types
of ambiguity in the sun and rain.
Its scholarly generosity on the fixed
blue stage however, matters little
to the June elder tree. Busy spreading
its many pearly palms onwards
and upwards, the green pinnate
universe seeks comfort in its white
constellations.
                    Out, secateurs! Out, human
hands! The secret ingredient (missing
in all recipes) is a dark cool cellar
where the flowers, canoodling
with the lemon zest, gradually translate
the language of love into the sparkling
forbearing quenching taste of summer.

YORKSHIRE GAZETTE, 1916: WAR-TIME ALLOTMENTS, PROMPT APPLICATIONS INVITED. The Parks Committee of the York Corporation have had under consideration the Board of Agriculture's Order in Council under the Defence of the Realm Act extending the existing powers of providing land for cultivation. We do not hesitate to say that the man who, knowing how to grow potatoes does not at once ask for land and get to work, will be as blameworthy as would the corporal who, seeing a chance to capture an army of the enemy, put off the effort until it was too late.

BRICKWORK

for Kate Weaver

The space gained by knocking
down the chimney might be vast
but the ghost of the soot lingering
in the naked kitchen is vaster
than any room or nose.
                    The natural
remedy is not exorcism but resurrection.
One by one, layer upon layer, they pile up
in the courtyard, waiting patiently
to be turned into new flowerbeds,
an iris pond with fern borders.
But the July sun is high on its mast
and no wonder the humans are all dead
tired, sleeping on their feet.
                      So, like
those bodies forsaken by the soul
and still expecting its return,
they will lie under the burning
sun and stay dry, red, and august
for weeks and weeks to come.

GENESIS 11:3: 'And they said one to another, Go to, let us make brick, and burn them
thoroughly. And they had brick for stone, and slime had they for mortar.'

69

Travelling at rail-speed the eye
anticipates the mind where
yellow fields after harvests yield a sky
of plain fatigue.
                    A nudge, a
certain inclination the train gives –
stopping as it starts, starting
as it stops: the transit stuttering
between despair and hope
supposed to keep you calm
and carry on, with or without
announcements. Punctuality is
a virtue, so is the resistance to it
in various forms. The faint tunes
of Regina Spektor, inquisitive hands
of young lovers, conversations
about politics and celebs, football
and alcohol,
                    what the living do
passing time when time just won't
pass.

REGINA SPEKTOR, BEGIN TO HOPE: 1 'Fidelity' 3:47 / 2 'Better' 3:22 / 3 'Samson' 3:10
/ 4 'On the Radio' 3:22 / 5 'Field Below' 5:18 / 6 ' Hotel Song' 3:29 / 7 'Après Moi' 5:08
/ 8 '20 Years of Snow' 3:31 / 9 'That Time' 2:39 / 10 'Edit' 4:53 / 11 'Lady' 4:45
/ 12 'Summer in the City' 3:50

RED-HANDED

for Amanda Lillie and Michael Fend

Of all the defences against
quotidian thievery in the name
of harvest, brambles keep by far
the best fences.
                        Between nettles
and tombstones their neighbourly
surveillance reinforces
September's prickly luxuriance.
Here a beloved husband kept
out of sight. There a stillborn
wrapped in black foliage.
How they adore the newly buried,
rooting through the ripe
plump, juicy flesh.
                        See!
How naturally I am picking
and choosing the mightier ones
over the sick and the poor. How
handful to jarful to shelfful
the end justifies the means.

MACBETH, 'The thane of Fife had a wife. Where is she now? – What, will these hands ne'er be clean? – No more o' that, my lord, no more o' that. You mar all with this starting.'

BOARDED-UP TREES

At the west corner of a junction
opposite an ex-Victorian pub
a bouquet of plane trees are boarded
up three years after Northern
Rock sank.
        Indisputably born
under an unlucky star, they did
what they could to green a grey
car park. From swimming pool
to casino to real estate, a derelict
piece of land lost to the human
instinct to plot and gain, even
at a loss. Decades of green shades
don't guarantee a green thought.
Think yellow,
        October, the cool
cautionary Fall that crisps everything
up. Above, the branches are fidgeting
in a form of bare defiance. Below,
some pedestrians crunching along
the pavement, ankle-deep in yellowness.

THE GUARDIAN, 14 September 2007: One woman, who did not wish to be named, told PA: 'I have withdrawn all my money. I got here at about 8.40am and was about 12th in the queue. It took me well over an hour to be served and by the time I got outside there must have been at least 50 people queuing out into the street.'

LIBRARY SCAFFOLDING

There is little reassurance even
in the land of strict alphabetical
order, when geometry in practice
is under the gale's sharpest
scrutiny.
                    Distraction walks through
the mind like a draft crossing
a room. Metals argue with the rain
and a hand nudges between the spines
fishing for a thought.
                            Asbestos,
the 'inextinguishable, unquenchable',
is quarantined on the upper floor
with Beethoven and Chopin
where the wind has stolen
the thunder from music.

Dr William Edmund Cooke, 'Fibrosis of the Lungs Due to the Inhalation of Asbestos Dust'. *BRITISH MEDICAL JOURNAL* (1924): 'A woman [Nellie Kershaw], aged 33 years, had worked in asbestos factories since the age of 13, but for five years previous to her finally ceasing work in July, 1922 her attendances at the factory had been intermittent. She died on March 15th, 1924. Mr. E. N. Molesworth, coroner for Rochdale, at the suggestion of Dr. Mackichan, who performed his necropsy, sent the lungs for further examination.'

WHITE ON WHITE

As each substance of a nothing
has twenty shadows, this fog
on cloud on snow is no less
than a blind spot in an absent
mind
       crossing
            out a figure
on an empty field no more
than one decimal place away, a
substance of a thing that has no
shadow but a yearlong full stop
rounding on and off December.

FARROW AND BALL'S WHITES: All White, Wimborne White, Pointing, Wevet, James White, Clunch, White Tie, New White, House White, Matchstick, Shadow White, Shaded White, Dimity, Joa's White, Lime White, Off White, Old White, Strong White, Cornforth White, Great White, Cabbage White. RICHARD II, 'Each substance of a grief hath twenty shadows'.

NOTES &
ACKNOWLEDGEMENTS

p. 26 'As Slow As Possible': John Cage's *ASLSP* is scheduled to run for 639 years, ending in 2640.

p. 28 'Ten Haikus by Fan Kuan': Fan Kuan (960-1030) painted 'Travellers Among Mountains and Streams' (山行旅).

p. 42 'Filial Piety' borrows from the Chinese saying: 樹欲靜而風不止 子欲養而親不待

p. 48 'The Painted Garden of the Villa of Livia' (30-20BC) had been reinstalled in the Palazzo Massimo alle Terme, Rome.

p. 53 'Genesis' is dedicated to my parents Lam Shing Ching 林瑞貞 and Fan Sheung Chung 范上中. Borrowing from the language of the authorised King James Bible, the poem is a collage, retelling legends and fables from Chinese creation myths. I thank the authors of the following sources which have made the collage possible:

> 袁珂:《中國古代神話》(北京: 中華書局, 1983)
> 許慎撰, 徐鉉校定:《說文解字附檢字》(北京: 中華書局, 2004)
> 李豐楙:《山海經》(臺北: 金楓出版社, 1987)
> 李學勤:《周易溯源》(成都: 巴蜀書社, 2006)
> 劉安:《淮南子》(台北: 台灣古籍出版有限公司, 2005)

I thank the editors of the following publications where earlier versions of these poems were printed: *Cha: An Asian Literary Journal, Eborakon, Literary Imagination, New Humanist, POEM, The London Magazine, The Poetry Review, Poetry Salzburg, Poetry Wales, Prairie Schooner, Voice and Verse, Yung Yang: A Journal of Hong Kong and International Writing.*

p. 15 'Transmigration' was shortlisted for the 2017 *TLS* Mick Imlah Poetry Prize and was published on the *TLS* website.

p. 18 'Among School Teachers' was published in *In Protest: 150 Poems for Human Rights* (Institute of English Studies, University of London, 2013) and in *Lacuna Magazine*. It is featured in *A Grain of Sand: Poems from Hong Kong*, a digital collection at the Chinese University of Hong Kong Library, produced by Mimi Ching: http://repository.lib.cuhk.edu.hk/en/collection/grainofsand

p. 35 'Don Kowloon' was published in *Quixotic: Poems East of La Mancha* (Chameleon Press, 2016) to commemorate the 400th anniversary of the death of Cervantes.

p. 38 'A Tree Ordained' was published in *Desde Hong Kong: Poets in Conversation with Octavio Paz* (Chameleon Press, 2015) to commemorate the centenary of the poet's birth.

p. 51 'Migrant' was published in the anthology *Wretched Strangers* edited by J T Welsch and Ágnes Lehóczky (Boiler House Press, 2018) to commemorate the anniversary of the June 2016 EU Referendum and in solidarity through struggles ongoing and to come. Proceeds of the book will be donated to charities fighting for the rights of refugees.

I thank John Wedgewood Clarke, Tony Ward, Angela Jarman, and the wonderful team at Arc Publications for making this book come to light and accommodating my fastidiousness with supernatural patience and earthly grace.

I thank Mimi Ching, Louise Ho, and Agnes Lam – my teachers who believed in me early on and taught me how to read with joy and self-scepticism.

I thank Adam Phillips for his enthusiasm for my poems, and for challenging me and reassuring me over the years.

I thank Alice Oswald and Fiona Sampson who heroically read the early manuscripts and helped me shape the book.

I thank Caitriona O'Reilly for her generous and meticulous reading of my poems and for being such a good poetry-companion.

I thank Ffiona Lewis for collaborating with me again and allowing
me to use her dazzling painting for the cover.

I thank Tammy Ho Lai-Ming and Jason Lee at the Hong Kong Baptist
University for connecting my work with the pulse of the changing city.

I thank Anna Armstrong, John Barnard, Lieven Clarisse, Judith
Clark, Ziad Elmarsafy, Michael Fend, Saskia Hamilton, Hermi-
one Lee, Hélène Lecossois, Amanda Lillie, Lorraine Ng, Jessica
Murray, Kabbie Ngo, Lionel Pilkington, Spencer Reece, Christine
Aronsen Storebo, Cyrus Tse, Kate & Geoffrey Weaver, and Polly
Yuen for their friendships and staying with me through peaks
and troughs.

And finally I thank Hugh, the first reader of these poems.

Kit Fan

Kit Fan was born in Hong Kong and moved to the UK at the age of 21. He studied at the Chinese University of Hong Kong before completing a doctoral thesis on Thom Gunn at the University of York. As well as being a published poet, he also writes fiction. In 2017 he was shortlisted for the *Guardian* 4th Estate BAME Short Story Prize for 'Duty Free' and the *TLS* Mick Imlah Poetry Prize.

In 2018 he won a Northern Writers' Award for *Diamond Hill*, a novel-in-progress portraying a deprived community in the last shanty town in Hong Kong being pushed to the point of collapse by property developers, Buddhist nuns, and the Triad during the dramatic period of accelerated development of the 1980s before the handover of the city from Britain to China in 1997.

His first book of poems *Paper Scissors Stone* won the inaugural HKU International Poetry Prize in 2011 and his translation of Classical Chinese poetry won one of the *Times* Stephen Spender Prizes in 2006.

He reviews regularly for *The Poetry Review*. As his poetry moves between Hong Kong and European cultural histories, he moves amphibiously between poetry and narrative fiction. He lives in York and works in the Hull York Medical School.